A CURE *for the* COMMON SCAM

A Non-Technical Guide for Navigating the Pitfalls of the Internet

Kyle Jekot, C.F.E.

ISBN 978-1-63630-027-6 (Paperback)
ISBN 978-1-63630-028-3 (Digital)

Covenant Books, Inc.
11661 Hwy 707
Murrells Inlet, SC 29576
www.covenantbooks.com

To my wife, Ashleigh, who is the love of my life. You are a reliable, caring, and amazing wife and mother to our children. I thank you for your continual support and encouragement as I chase all my fantastically random hopes and dreams. It would be hard to imagine how I've navigated through this life without you.

To my kids, Brynn, Jackson, and Sawyer, it is difficult for me to put into words how you've shaped my life today, and all I can say for that is thank you. I wouldn't want to go through life without our times of laughter, dodge ball, and living room dance parties.

To Ashleigh, Brynn, Jackson, and Sawyer, my crew.

CONTENTS

ACKNOWLEDGEMENTS

It took some time for me to realize that it isn't easy to sit down and write a book. You can have a hundred ideas and topics you want to cover, but putting them into a meaningful and sensible format that is easy to follow is a real art. I could not have done this without the many reviewers, friends whom I ran ideas past, gathered stories from, and received assistance from through this process. Those people who read through my initial manuscript, as well as the many needed revisions, made this book what it is today.

When I first came up with the idea for this book and had the first manuscript drafted, I went to an excellent friend, Adam, and asked him to read it and give me feedback. He said to me, "I'd be honored, but I'm no tech expert." My response was, "*Perfect!*" because my goal in writing this book is to provide a non-technical approach to, at times, complicated topics. So, to you, Adam, for your friendship, brotherhood, and eagle eye for detail.

To Scotti, my cousin, godfather, and English professor, all wrapped into one, your countless edits, revisions, and recommendations made this book better in so many ways. I don't know what else to say but thank you.

Finally, and most importantly, thank you to God for giving me the ability to write this book and the opportunity to share my stories. God has put me in many different life situations that have challenged me and my faith, knowing that he was in control through it all. I am grateful that he has bestowed so many blessings of love, kindness, and mercy on me throughout my life.

INTRODUCTION

My goal for this book is to provide non-technical and easily understandable concepts and techniques to keep you and your loved ones financially and technologically safe when navigating the Internet. According to a 2018 survey, more than sixty-six percent of Americans over the age of sixty-five were active on the Internet[1]. That is why this book is so important, as it will guide you, the reader, through common pitfalls scammers and hackers will use to take advantage of unsuspecting or untrained individuals. While this book and the techniques described within it cannot guarantee you will be safe on the Internet, I will provide some realistic tactics and solutions to typical schemes of scammers and hackers who will try to compromise your accounts.

Many of the concepts and techniques discussed in this book will attempt to strike a balance between security and convenience. As an example, it is very convenient to use the word *"password"* to secure an account. By using a simplistic password, however, you are under-emphasizing security and making

---

[1]   https://www.pewresearch.org/internet/2017/05/17/tech-adoption-climbs-among-older-adults/

your accounts easy targets for scammers and hackers to compromise and potentially steal your personal and confidential information. Conversely, you could create a password that is a combination of uppercase and lowercase letters, characters, and numbers that looks something like this: *RP?jC@mAFNJAp9!db@ w2$#L#fcFjc_cH+*. While I am reasonably confident that using a password like the example above would secure your personal information and make it difficult, if not impossible, for a scammer or hacker to infiltrate your account, who would ever want to regularly use or even try to remember a complex password such as this? That is why it is essential when implementing the concepts discussed in this book to strike a balance between security and convenience and maintain your comfort level between the two.

THE CATALYST

You may ask me, why are you writing this book? I fall into the category of what some in society today call a 'xennial,' a group that bridges the gap between Generation X and the Millennials. Xennials are often characterized as being born into an analog childhood and transitioning into a digital adulthood. As someone who grew up playing endless games like MathBlaster and Mavis Beacon Teaches Typing in a computer lab in my elementary school, to witnessing the infancy of the Internet with the America Online '100 Free Hours!' CDs that would come in the mail regularly to enjoying streaming my favorite TV series on my laptop, I've learned the hard way the common traps and pitfalls that reign throughout cyberspace, a potential consequence of everyday, seemingly innocuous activities. I've learned not only tough lessons through these incidents but also the remediation steps that one must take to re-secure one's computer and personal information.

I vividly recall an incident when I was fourteen years old. I was on the family computer writing a high school report when a box popped up on the computer monitor that I didn't recognize. In this box, a hacker was communicating with me and said, "Hey, I'm in your computer, want to see something cool?" I didn't know how to respond at the time because I was admittedly a little confused as to what was happening, so I didn't respond to his question. He then asked if I wanted to see the Start button on my screen disappear. About five seconds later, the Start button vanished from the taskbar! I had no idea where the Start button went, how the hacker did this, or probably most importantly, how I could get this hacker out of our computer. I didn't even know at the time that you could remove the Start button from the taskbar! He then told me that he had all my father's banking and credit card information. So, in a confused panic, I did the only thing I knew how to do at the time—I unplugged the phone cord (yes, no Wi-Fi around this time) from the wall to disconnect the Internet connection. I'll show you who's the boss, hacker! Ah, *sweet revenge*!

Except that vengeful delight was short-lived since, to prevent further access to our network and personal information, we had to permanently wipe the whole computer and reinstall all the programs to ensure that the software the hacker installed to remotely connect was eliminated.

More recently, I received a call from my wife's aunt and uncle, who told me that they received a call from a major technology company, informing them of the need to update their software package or lose all their personal information. They subsequently gave the technology 'representative' (using this term loosely, of course) full access to their computer. Then, when it was time to pay for his 'services,' my wife's aunt and uncle used a third-party vendor to pay $85.00 for the "update." When they explained all of this to me, my face fell into my hands because I immediately recognized, based on my previous knowledge and experience, several red flags that would indicate that my wife's aunt and uncle were victims of a scam. This situation taught me a critical lesson about the society that we live in today, especially for generations that did not grow up with the Internet. Identification of suspicious circumstances and situations, while paramount to keeping yourself safe online, may not always be apparent to the inexperienced eye.

DISCLAIMER

A reminder, there are no methods or techniques currently available to completely prevent your identity from being stolen. The contents of this book provide best practices, suggestions, and/or recommendations to keeping you and your identity safe, but the author assumes no responsibility or liability in the event of identity theft despite using the techniques described herein.

PASSWORDS

Treat your password like a toothbrush. Don't let anybody else use it and replace it every six months. (Clifford Stoll, American astronomer)

The password is the distinct first line of defense for any account, and as the first line of defense, it is imperative they are complex, unique, and able to withstand attempts by scammers and hackers from infiltrating your personal accounts. The password acts as the first key to your information. To show what not to do, here are the top ten most used passwords according to a 2018 survey[2]:

1. 123456
2. password
3. 123456789
4. 12345678
5. 12345

---

[2] https://www.welivesecurity.com/2018/12/17/most-popular-passwords-2018-revealed/

6. 111111
7. 1234567
8. sunshine
9. qwerty
10. iloveyou

Frankly, these are incredibly problematic passwords because they lack the complexity and unique-
ness that keep your account secure. They all follow a similar pattern and are more than likely used
across logins, meaning once a scammer or hacker
figures out the password, they will try it with other
accounts. Despite these issues, these oversimplified
passwords—and others like them—are nonetheless
used every day by millions of people around the
world. A primary reason behind this was discussed
at the beginning of this book: convenience often
outweighs security when an individual creates a password. However, think for a moment, of the potentially detrimental consequences of a scammer or
hacker gaining access to your account. According to
a report by InfoArmor, a company that specializes in
identity theft protection, depending on the complexity of an identity theft event, it can take between one
hundred to two hundred hours and up to *six* months
to repair the damage done by having your identity
stolen[3]. Most of us simply do not have the time to go
through and repair the damage done by having one
or more of our accounts compromised.

---

[3] https://blog.infoarmor.com/employees/time-correct-
identity-fraud-steps-protection

Surprisingly, given the weak passwords described above, password complexity and security are undoubtedly on the mind of most Americans. A study done by Experian revealed that nearly seventy-three percent of consumers say that they are "very or somewhat concerned their e-mail, financial accounts, or social media could be hacked." What is disconcerting, however, is that the same study showed only fifty-three percent of respondents stated that they take additional precautions to protect their Internet presence[4]. That's like saying I want to lose weight so my clothes fit better, but I don't want to diet or go to the gym to achieve the anticipated results. For this reason, you should take the steps not only described in strengthening your password but implement as many additional measures as available to protect yourself from identity theft.

Many websites today provide suggestions to increase the strength of passwords, and some won't let you continue until you create a stronger password. At a minimum, I would recommend adhering to those website-generated password requirements as often as possible. It is important to remember the components of a strong password.

---

[4] https://www.experian.com/blogs/ask-experian/americans-worried-about-identity-theft-unlikely-to-protect-themselves-survey/

Length

Scammers and hackers typically use what is known as a 'brute force attack' by using a computer script to identify and test a set combination of numbers, letters, and symbols against a login ID and password until it ascertains the password. By increasing both the length and complexity of the password, the process takes longer for the script to decipher your password. While there is no general rule of how long a password should be, I tend to use passwords that are a variation of letters, numbers, and symbols that are at least sixteen characters long. Now, you might ask, "How am I supposed to remember a password that is sixteen characters long that contains letters, symbols, and numbers?" In the next section, we will describe how the substitution of symbols for letters and numbers will allow you to make a password that's memorable and appropriately complex.

Variations of Letters, Symbols, and Numbers

Let's look at the eighth most common password above: sunshine. Using a search engine, you can find many websites that allow you to run a 'test' password through them to see how long it could take for a scammer or hacker to figure out your password. These websites use an algorithm that defines the time required, from 'instantly' to 'millions of years,' to decipher a password based on the complexity and length. In our example, according to one of our test websites, sunshine is an 'instantly' decipherable password. Meanwhile, let's say you used a variation of sunshine like this:

sunshine ➔ *$uNsh!n3*

Using the variations of letters, numbers, and symbols in place of the regular spelling of even a simple word like this increases the time it would take the supercomputer to figure out your password from 'instantly' to 'nine hours!' Not bad at all for just substituting a few characters and numbers for letters. Now, let's add two additional characters to our new password:

$uNsh!n3 ➔ *$uNsh!n3:)*

By adding two characters to our new password, in this case, a smiley face—because, after all, who doesn't love sunshine?—it increases the time necessary to crack this password from nine hours to fifty-three years! One additional consideration is adding spaces within your password. As the importance of password complexity increases, many websites will now allow you to use a space as a character in your password. So, for our last example, let's take our password that would take fifty-three years to crack and add a space somewhere in the password:

$uNsh!n3:) ➔ *$uNsh !n3:)*

Running our new password with the space included in our test password algorithm now increases the time to crack from fifty-three years to—are you ready for this?—five thousand years! Simply by adding a space in the password!

Making these simple changes, we took the eighth most common password, which a hacker could instantly crack, and increased the time it would take to break it to five thousand years! Applying these same techniques of character variation will exponentially increase the safety of your account.

Using Personal Information

We will talk about this later in the book, but with the number of breaches of personal information in society today between credit bureaus and corporations large and small, you are asking for trouble if your password contains any personal information, including names of pets, children, or spouses. Your password should not provide any information that would be readily available in your credit report, social media, or general Internet presence. Scammers and hackers will often research information that is both publicly available as well as information obtained through illicit means, such as credit reporting and corporate breaches. You may ask, how do scammers and hackers have access to this information from security breaches? Often, that information is on what is known as the 'Deep Web' and/or the 'Dark Web.'

While these two terms are frequently used inter-changeably, they are two different things.

When explaining the Internet or Surface Web, Deep Web, and Dark Web, the image often suggested to visualize is that of a glacier.

Typically, an estimated ninety percent of a gla-cier's volume and mass is underwater and unseen from the surface. In much the same way, the Deep Web and the Dark Web, which is a subset of the Deep Web, operate in very much the same fashion. The Surface Web includes your everyday Google search, Wikipedia article, and YouTube video. The Deep Web, meanwhile, consists of websites that cannot be found by traditional search engines, and as such, and without going into too much technical detail, there are specific parameters and information that must be known to access these areas of the Internet. It is within the Dark Web, where the illicit activity often occurs, including the purchasing and exchanging of personally identifiable information for use in gaining unauthorized access to accounts. By creating passwords that cannot be easily recreated or identified through your personal information, you are making it more difficult for the scammer or hacker to gain access to your account illegally.

Do Not Reuse Passwords

The reusing of passwords is a hacker's dream, primarily because they only must figure out the password and can test all your other accounts to see which of them use the same password. I fully understand how difficult and time-consuming it is to remember unique passwords for each account, but your account security and your personal information and identity are far too valuable to reuse passwords over multiple accounts. In the next section, we will describe the use of password vaults, which will assist you in remembering all your new, incredibly unique, and complex passwords!

Password Sharing

What I am about to say should not come as a shock to you, but in the interest of over-communication and reiteration, don't share your passwords with anyone else and be aware of your surroundings when you are entering account information to prevent an unauthorized individual from looking over your shoulder. Also, don't save actual password information in a Word or Notepad document on your computer. As an alternative solution, save a document that only contains hints and not the actual password and save it as something that is nondescript and doesn't scream, "Here are all my passwords hackers!" Also, you may want to password-protect this document for extra security. I strongly recommend, however, that, if you are going to go through the trouble of keeping all your passwords in a Word document, simply use a password vault instead, which will give you increased security.

Password versus Passphrase

You may hear the words password and passphrase used interchangeably, but these are actually two different methods for securing an account. The primary difference between these two words is that a passphrase is generally longer and is comprised of a random set of words. In most instances, a passphrase will still meet the required parameters of websites because they contain words, letters, and symbols. Additionally, and probably more beneficially, passphrases are easier to remember because they are not made of a random smattering of upper- and lowercase, symbols, and numbers. If we run a passphrase through the same algorithm above, for example, the passphrase, *"Golf.Runner.Dime1!"* it would take the supercomputer three hundred eighty quadrillion years to crack this password! That's fifteen zeroes! It is important to remember, however, that the words chosen for a passphrase must be random to increase the effectiveness of the passphrase itself.

Frequency of Password Changes

While there is no official timeframe for how often you should change your passwords, some security professionals will suggest that every password should be changed every six months. This should occur on a more frequent basis, however, if you have reason to believe your accounts are compromised. I would suggest following the advice of the American astronomer quoted at the beginning of this chapter and change every six months—oh, and get yourself a new toothbrush too while you're at it!

COMMON SCAMS
TODAY

Trust your instinct to the end,
though you can render no reason.
(Ralph Waldo Emerson)

Telltale Signs of a Fraudulent E-mail

Let's face it, most of the e-mail that we receive today is junk. Between the e-mails telling me of a thirty percent off *everything* sale to free trials of software I'll never use, looking through your e-mail can be an exhausting endeavor. Can you imagine for a second if e-mail didn't exist and we only received traditional junk mail, which we still get today anyway? The physical mailboxes at the end of driveways would be overflowing! Now, let's say, however, as you are sorting through all that junk e-mail, you come across a strange e-mail that says, "We're updating our records, please confirm your information!" You open the e-mail, and at first glance, it has all the makings of a legitimate e-mail, so you have no reason to suspect otherwise. The company logo looks right, and the e-mail text looks right too, so you click on the box in the e-mail that says 'Verify My Info," and *bam*!—just like that, you've inadvertently installed malicious software, or 'malware' as it's commonly called, onto your computer.

This technique is known as 'spear phishing,' and it is a lucrative method of fraud. Each day, approximately one hundred fifty-six million phishing e-mails are sent around the globe[5]. Of that, 80,000 people fall victim to a phishing scam by providing personal information to an individual who is looking to commit fraud. So, don't be embarrassed if you get 'phished' because you are most certainly not alone!

Let's look at the example below from an actual phishing e-mail my wife received. On the surface and after a quick read, it seems like a legitimate e-mail; it has the company logo, and if we don't act now, our account will be disabled, and information erased! Before anything else though, your first step should be to stop and take a breath.

---

[5] https://www.uspsoig.gov/document/information-security-awareness-training-and-phishing

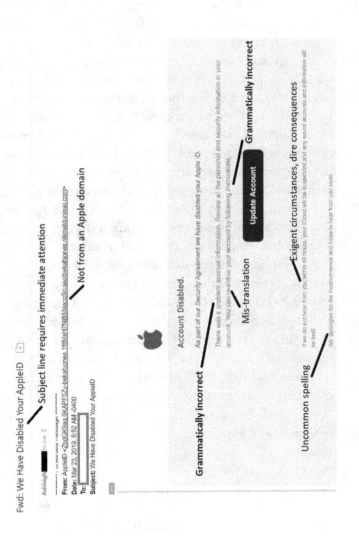

Fwd: We Have Disabled Your AppleID

Ashleigh ___ to me

From: AppleID <ZbdGiK9an_8KAPF5Xz-betahomes.1t8Ms4i7N9MJaaocSti.sestbekahones.nkmaldunjau.com>
Date: Mar 23, 2019, 8:52 AM -0400
To:
Subject: We Have Disabled Your AppleID

Subject line requires immediate attention

Not from an Apple domain

Account Disabled.

As part of our Security Agreement we have disabled your Apple ID.

There was a problem account information. Review all the personal and security information in your account. You can re-active your account by following instructions.

Update Account

Grammatically incorrect

Mis-translation

Exigent circumstances, dire consequences

If we do not hear from you within 48 hours, your iCloud will be suspended and any saved accounts and information will be lost!

We apologise for the inconvenience and hope to hear from you soon.

Uncommon spelling

Grammatically incorrect

First, let's look at the subject line of the e-mail, "We have disabled your AppleID"—this is meant to draw your attention, and instinctively, you will want to do whatever is necessary to re-enable your ID as quickly as possible. As you read through, however, you notice a few things that seem out of place. First, in looking at who sent the e-mail, it indicates that it is from 'AppleID,' but the domain or the e-mail address it was sent from is a combination of letters and numbers and does not correlate to an Apple domain, such as AppleIDSupport@apple.com as an example.

In the body of the e-mail, you will also notice that several sentences are grammatically incorrect. The first sentence is missing a few words and should read, "There was a problem *with your* account information." Further down, there are mistranslations (e.g. re-active should be reactivate), as well as uncommon spellings (e.g. apologise should be apologize), and most importantly, exigent circumstances and consequences of inaction. The exigent circumstances play on the e-mail recipient's psyche, and if the account is disabled within forty-eight hours and account information will be erased, it is more likely the e-mail recipient will hastily click on the "Update Account" button, which will probably install some form of malware onto the recipient's computer. To further investigate the legitimacy of such communications, you can also hover over the 'Update Account' button (do *not* click!), and most often, it will not correspond to anything related to the vendor on the e-mail.

Customer Support

------ Forwarded message ------
From: Amazon <service.fuppqtc@GTTp3Ilg1.co> The email sender is not from an Amazon email address (e.g.
support@amazon.com)
Date: Jan 2, 2020, 9:45 AM 0500
To:
Subject: Locked   Subject line shows a sense of urgency

Time sensitive request, dire consequences of inaction

Dear Customer,
We have faced some problems with your account. So Please update your account details. If you do not update your account within 24 hours (from opening this email) will be officially permanently disabled.

Grammatically incorrect

[Update Now]

We hope to see you again soon.
Amazon.com

Here is another example where we can use the techniques described above to determine if this is a legitimate e-mail or not. This is another e-mail my wife received from a scammer portraying themselves as Amazon customer service:

A review of the e-mail address does not show a typical support or customer service e-mail address, but rather an unintelligible combination of letters and numbers. The subject line of the e-mail, "Locked," is enough to be intriguing and piquing of one's curiosity to open the e-mail to see what is locked at Amazon. Within the body of the e-mail, we see multiple grammatically incorrect errors and misplaced punctuation. Finally, as with the other e-mail example, the scammer plays on the recipient's emotions by indicating they must act within twenty-four hours or their account will be permanently disabled, which shows the dire consequences of inaction.

In situations such as these, it is essential to take a step back, review the e-mail, and look for the red flags identified above. By taking this step back, you are more likely to notice items that seem incorrect, suspicious, or out of place. I'll mention this several times as you read, but as much as it is imperative to identify possible red flags, trusting your instincts and not proceeding if something does not feel right is just as important.

Unsolicited Calls

As I mentioned at the beginning of this book, my wife's aunt and uncle were victims of a scammer who posed as technical support for a major technology company. Unfortunately, because they did not know any better and the scammer knew precisely what to say, they gave the scammer full access to their computer and even paid the scammer $85.00 through a third-party vendor for his "assistance." Through the course of the conversation, the scammer told them their products needed to be updated, and if they didn't update the software, their computer would crash, and they would lose everything.

You can see, like the e-mail above, the scammers and hackers prey on exigency and dire circumstances of inaction. Once the scammer was inside their computer, he installed malware to regain access to their computer later. As a result of this incident, unfortunately, I had to wipe their entire computer and reinstall all their programs to remove the malware successfully. This was an unfortunate yet preventable incident if you know the red flags of a situation like this. Some key takeaways from this incident:

1. Unless you contact them first, it is highly unlikely major technology carriers will contact you to assist with any technical support. If the caller leaves you a voicemail with a number to call back, the first thing you should do is look up the phone number

from which they called in a search engine such as Google or Bing. Most of the time, if it is a scammer or hacker impersonating a vendor or business, they will be calling from a phone number that another person who received a similar call documented the identity of the caller and may have already flagged it as a scammer.

2. In the situation above, most major technology carriers are large enough that they have no need to process transactions through a third-party vendor like PayPal and can independently process credit card transactions. If you receive a call asking for you to send money via a third-party vendor, there's an excellent chance someone is trying to scam you.

3. The scammer will often be quite pushy and play upon your emotions of fear and confusion in the situation. Arming yourself with these techniques will help you to resist that urge to cooperate with them and as a result, will keep you and your accounts and personal information safe.

4. If something doesn't feel right, it probably isn't right. There's nothing wrong with hanging up and blocking the number.

Family Member in Trouble

I heard of another incident recently where a gentleman from my local church received a call stating that the police arrested his grandson in another state, and if he didn't make bail, his grandson was going to prison. In this example too, we can see exactly how the scammers again prey on the emotions and exigency of the circumstances to induce a person to act quickly and without contemplation. The gentleman was considered by many to be very sharp, but his feelings got the best of him, and he sent the person who he initially thought was a police department money to bail his grandson out of jail. He later said that he sat up all night thinking about what happened and how the whole situation just seemed 'off' to him. He contacted his bank the next day and stopped the transfer just before it reached the scammers. In the end, he trusted his instinct and gut feeling about the situation and saved himself from being scammed.

The key takeaways are mostly the same as the incident with my aunt and uncle, but this scenario is slightly more concerning because it relies on the supposed premise of a family member who is in trouble. Presumably, without proper guidance and knowledge, most of us would probably react in the same manner this gentleman did. In both situations, despite the scammer's attempts to push the target into action, it was vital to take a step back, analyze the situation, and proceed from there. Again, there is nothing wrong with hanging up the phone on them and blocking the number.

Social Security/IRS Calls

As your personal information becomes more and more available, one up and coming scam around tax time involves an individual receiving a call from someone purporting to be from the IRS. In this scam, the scammer displays all the supposed trappings of an actual IRS agent. They will tell you their badge number, their location, and the department within the IRS in which they work to further legitimize the scam. They will tell you that you are delinquent on your tax payments, and you must pay them using a gift card or wire transfer or risk going to prison. But we know better! As is outlined on the IRS website[6], they will not do the following:

- Call and demand payment immediately, primarily via a gift card or wire transfer. More likely, the IRS will send you a tax bill through the US Postal Service,
- Threaten to bring in local law enforcement to arrest you for non-compliance,
- Demand payment without an appeal process of the amount of money owed, and
- Specifically request for credit or debit card numbers over the phone.

[6] https://www.irs.gov/newsroom/how-to-know-its-really-the-irs-calling-or-knocking-on-your-door

If you do receive one of these calls, you can rest assured that it is most likely not the IRS calling you and can hang up on the scammer. Still, you can see from the tactics employed here that they all tend to follow a similar pattern of increasing the necessity of compliance or facing dire consequences, requiring you to act on emotion instead of a logical thought process. Do not let them attempt to rattle you, no matter how hard they push or how agitated they become.

ACCOUNT VERIFICATION SECURITY QUESTIONS

"Doveryai no proveryai"—
Russian proverb, translated as,
'Trust, but verify."

In the popular ABC Network sitcom *Modern Family*, Gloria Pritchett inadvertently sends an e-mail to Claire Dunphy, her stepdaughter, explaining that she doesn't want to work at a school bake sale because Claire is a "bossy control freak who looks down on my cupcakes, even though your lemon squares were very dry." In trying to retrieve the e-mail before Claire reads it, Gloria goes to Claire's house to access her computer and delete the e-mail. While at Claire's house, Gloria runs into Phil, Claire's husband, and the conversation follows:

Gloria: I was sending an e-mail to my brother in Colombia. I was telling him about Claire. You know, I realized there's so much I don't know about her. Like, for example, what is her favorite word? Or what was her first pet's name?

Phil: I'm not an idiot. Are you trying to get Claire's password?

Gloria: Okay fine. I sent her something by mistake. I need to get into Claire's e-mail to erase it before she sees it.

This is a classic example of Gloria attempting to use what is known as social engineering, using deception to manipulate individuals into providing confidential information, in an attempt to ascertain Claire's password. I would say though, that, with the number of company security breaches, especially the Equifax breach, account verification security questions are probably the least safe method of authenticating and securing your account. For a scammer or hacker with access to stolen information about you, it could be straightforward for them to figure out the answers to questions such as the first street you grew up on or the name of your high school. Accordingly, to use this security function effectively, you must get creative in how you answer these questions.

I used to work with a gentleman who was brilliant when it came to security. There was a time where we were working on a project and he had to reset an account. So, he called our help desk, and they asked him, "To verify your account, can you please tell me your mother's maiden name?" He looked at me and started to chuckle before he answered, "Niagara Falls," with some excitement (and possible embarrassment) in his voice. That was, in fact, the correct answer, and he reset his password.

After he got off the phone, I asked him why he chose the phrase Niagara Falls for his mother's maiden name. He said, and he was right, there's no requirement that you must answer these security questions truthfully. The questions are designed for easy recollection if needed. However, this recall also plays to the advantage of a scammer or hacker who may be trying to access your account. Companies who use account verification security questions are not reviewing them, saying, "Your dog is not named Ford Thunderbird, please provide his real name." Again, it just must be something memorable that you can recall if asked. In his example, he said that he doesn't focus on his mother's maiden name but the location where she got married, which was Niagara Falls. A mother's maiden name would be relatively easy to decipher through Internet searches and illicitly obtained information, but the city of where she got married would be significantly more challenging to guess for a scammer or hacker.

Another solution to answering account security questions is to choose the questions that may be more obscure and difficult to guess or figure out from social media or your online presence. For example, it would be a more significant challenge for a scammer or hacker to guess the first movie you saw in theaters or the name of your first grade teacher than to guess your mother's maiden name or the name of your first street.

BANK SAFETY

> *Corruption, embezzlement, fraud, these are all characteristics which exist everywhere. It is regrettably the way human nature functions, whether we like it or not. What successful economies do is keep it to a minimum. No one has ever eliminated any of that stuff. (Alan Greenspan)*

I've spent most of my career in both the financial services industry and law enforcement where I've gained a wealth of knowledge and experience when it comes to fraud and its corresponding red flags that seem to grow in intricacy and complexity daily. There is, unfortunately, no shortage of scams and schemes to trick, pressure, and cajole unsuspecting or unwitting people into these fraud schemes. It is, however, given me an equally unique insight to put tools and techniques in place and communicate these methods to others so that (hopefully!) the number of people that fall victim to these scams is significantly reduced.

In 2018, Bloomberg reported a staggering number regarding fraud and America's elderly. In 2018 alone, America's elderly lost $37 billion due to fraud[7]. *Billion*, with a B! In 2019, the Consumer Financial Protection Bureau reported the average losses by age range as a result of fraud[8]:

- 70–79 → $45,300
- 80 and older → $39,200
- 60–69 → $22,700
- 50–59 → $13,400

This statistical breakdown clearly exemplifies why scammers and hackers tend to target those above the age of seventy, as it is the most lucrative age range for fraud. In the same 2019 study, scammers and hackers initiated over fifty-one percent of the fraud incidents against individuals they did not personally know.

Micro-Deposits and Micro-Withdrawals

Reviewing your monthly statement can help you identify potential problems with your accounts before they become more significant problems. One common tactic for scammers and hackers to use is the concept of micro-deposits and micro-withdraw-

---

[7] https://www.bloomberg.com/news/features/2018-05-03/america-s-elderly-are-losing-37-billion-a-year-to-fraud

[8] https://www.aarp.org/money/scams-fraud/info-2019/cfpb-report-financial-elder-abuse.html

als. In the financial service industry, micro-deposits can serve an essential and necessary function to authenticate a person's account. Many of the third-party vendors that process transactions will send you a micro-deposit, typically between $0.01 and $0.10. When you receive those micro-deposits, the vendor will ask for the specific amounts of the micro-deposits, which will, in turn, prove that you have access to the account you are trying to link with the third-party service. The vendor considers this an added level of protection and security to verify the user of the bank account.

But if you have micro-deposits on your account and you aren't trying to set up a new account with a payment vendor, then your account may have been compromised.

Often, scammers and hackers will use micro-deposits and micro-withdrawals to verify if an account is active before attempting to make a more substantial withdrawal or purchase. By 'testing' the account first, it prevents the victim from noticing that their account has been compromised unless a regular statement review is completed on an ongoing basis. Since the population that balances a checkbook anymore is small or potentially non-existent, completing a statement review on a pre-determined basis, say, monthly, will allow you to identify odd or suspicious transactions before they become an issue.

If you do have micro-deposits or micro-withdrawals on your bank statement and you haven't opened any new accounts, or no reason exists for such transactions, you should contact your bank and have a new account created, as your current account has likely been compromised.

Suspicious Transactions

As you complete your statement review, it is also imperative that you identify any other suspicious transactions that you do not recall making. Historically speaking, scammers and hackers utilized a 'one and done' approach for unauthorized transactions. This technique entails the scammer or hacker making one large purchase and 'burning the account,' making further use of the account difficult, as the account owner may notice a large withdrawal or transaction in short order.

What began to happen recently, however, is that scammers and hackers will now utilize smaller account transactions over a more extended period to draw less suspicion to their deeds. Since a fair amount of the population does not do a regular statement review, $20.00 or $30.00 may not attract as much attention as suspicious activity in someone's account, and would allow the fraud to be drawn out of an extended period of time compared to a $500.00 purchase. Many banks today offer fraud notifications and alerts for suspicious transactions, including micro-deposits, micro-withdrawals, and suspicious transactions or activities. My recommendation is to enable every possible fraud alert provided on your bank accounts. Yes, you may get more alerts than you would typically care to read, but it will at least give you peace of mind from being scammed because of the timely identification of possible suspicious activity.

ONLINE SHOPPING

We see our customers as invited guests to a party, and we are the hosts. It's our job every day to make every important aspect of the customer experience a little bit better. (Jeff Bezos)

It is safe to say that the Internet has revolutionized the way we shop today. It has brought about some of the downfall and closure of some of the biggest names in the retail industry. It's easy to see why the explosion of online shopping has driven so many big names out of the market: it's convenient and always accessible. We've even come to the point where we have Cyber Monday, a whole day dedicated solely to online shopping and "can't-miss" deals. But just how safe is online shopping? Studies show that the number one reason why people like to shop online is that you can shop at all hours of the day[9]. The same survey showed that sixty-five percent of people would

[9] https://www.smartinsights.com/ecommerce/ecommerce-strategy/the-reasons-why-consumers-shop-online-instead-of-in-stores/

do comparison pricing for a product online while standing in a physical store. Finally, in 2018, online shoppers accounted for over $517 billion in sales[10]. Online shopping will only continue to grow in our society, so we must take the proper precautions to secure ourselves while online.

Is the website who they really say they are?

Scammers will, at times, create websites that make it difficult to determine whether they are the genuine retail sites that users intend to visit. They will invest significant amounts of time into creating these fake websites in the hopes that the links you click on will install malware onto your computer that will steal your personal information. But there are steps we can take that will combat their efforts to steal your information.

Navigating directly to the website

Most of the time, we stumble upon websites created by hackers as a result of looking up a company through a search engine like Google. According to a 2010 study, hackers were creating, on average, 57,000 fake websites every week[11], and building them in such a way that they would appear higher in

---

[10] https://www.digitalcommerce360.com/article/us-ecommerce-sales/

[11] https://phys.org/news/2010-09-hackers-booby-trapped-websites-weekly-experts.html

search engine results, in the hopes that unsuspecting victims would click on their links and subsequently have their information stolen through malware installation or website impersonation. In most instances, we can avoid this trap by navigating directly to the website instead of using the search engine.

Understandably, if you aren't sure of what the exact URL of the site is, you would need to use a search engine to confirm, but if, say we knew we were going to Amazon, navigating directly to amazon.com is far safer than trying to find the link through a Google search.

Now, let's say that you must use a search engine to find the correct name of a website; how can we be sure that the site is legitimate and not a website set up by a scammer hoping to steal your information? The first place to start is in the address bar at the top. Most, if not all, legitimate websites will display two critical items in the address bar that will confirm that they are official websites: https and a padlock icon.

Https, or HyperText Transfer Protocol Secure, is a method by which a website authenticates the integrity, protection, and privacy of the data transferred between your computer and the site you are navigating. More importantly, https confirms the trustworthiness of a website.

With all https websites, you will also see a padlock icon next to the address bar. The padlock is a secondary verification that the site you are on is legitimate, and you can safely navigate there. In 2017, the Google Chrome browser also implemented the words

"Not Secure" for all websites that are not secured through https to alert the user to be mindful of entering personal information and navigating through the site. Additionally, there are security features within some anti-virus software packages that scan a website and provide you with a checkmark next to the link in your search engine results to identify websites that are legitimate and others that may be suspicious. As an example, the anti-virus software I personally use does a verification check of a website and places a green checkmark next to the URL to indicate that it is a legitimate website, as shown below when I search for Amazon:

⊘ Amazon.com: Online Shopping for Electronics, Apparel ...
https://www.amazon.com ▾
Free One-Day Delivery on millions of items with Prime. Low prices across earth's biggest selection of books, music, DVDs, electronics, computers, software, ...

Alternative Solutions to Using a Credit Card

There are times when we find ourselves in a situation where we aren't a hundred percent comfortable with making an online purchase. Let's say your grandson wants an obscure toy from a website that does not appear to be completely legitimate, and your gut instinct is making you a bit wary to input your bank account information into their online order form. You've gone through the checks, and everything about the site *seems* okay, but still, just something doesn't feel right. There's nowhere else where this toy is available, so you want to go through with the purchase. How can you protect yourself from falling victim to a scam or having a hacker steal your personal information?

In full disclosure, what I am about to describe can be a bit of a time-consuming effort, but this is one of the safest ways to shop online when buying from sites that you feel may or may not be legitimate. So, let's say you figure out that the purchase price, tax, and shipping of your grandson's 'has to have' toy is $56.00. What you can do is go to any local store that sells gift cards and buy one that has the credit card logo (e.g., Visa or Mastercard) with cash for $60.00. By paying with cash, there's no information about your bank account information that could be attached to the gift card that a potential hacker could steal. Since the gift card has a Visa label, the vendor *should* accept the payment without any issues. If the worst-case scenario occurs and a scammer or hacker attempts to steal your personal information from the card, the only information they could obtain is your shipping address and the remaining balance, if any, on the gift card. As I mentioned, this is a bit of an extreme scenario and process, but it is a very effective way of protecting yourself during online shopping.

TECHNICAL
CONSIDERATIONS

*Tell me and I forget. Teach
me and I remember. Involve me
and I learn. (Benjamin Franklin)*

I know that I mentioned in the beginning this is a non-technical guide for navigating the Internet, but the purpose of this section is to provide some techniques that will provide additional layers of defense against scammers and hackers. I purposefully saved this section for the end of the book, not because I think it's less important—in fact, quite the opposite. I explained, in the beginning, that this is a non-technical guide to safely navigating the jungle known as the Internet. Accordingly, I did not want the first section of the book to be a highly technical overview of methods to employ when there are other important and decidedly less technical solutions to implement to keep yourself safe online.

You should view your Internet safety and protection as concentric circles with you and your personal information in the center. All these circles provide a layer of defense that, when all working together at the same time, will significantly reduce potential instances of having your identity stolen, computer hacked, and other negative impacts from the Internet. To that end, Two-Factor Authentication, Virtual Private Networks, computer and anti-virus software updates are all crucial in the concentric circles of securing your online presence.

Two-Factor Authentication

Two-Factor Authentication, or 2FA as it is commonly referred to, can best be described as something you know, something you have, or something you are. These concepts break down in the following way:

- Something that you know—Your password, PIN, zip code, answer to a security question (first movie seen in theatres, first car, etc.)
- Something that you have—A cell phone or a fob that generates a code you can input
- Something that you are—Biometric screening such as fingerprint, face, or voice

2FA uses two of these three methods to authenticate you as the owner of an account. In most cases, such as your e-mail, your provider will use something that you know plus something that you have methods to verify you as the user. You may also hear the phrase Multi-Factor Authentication, or MFA, which means you are using more than two methods of authentication.

Let's take your e-mail as an example. When you log in, you type in your e-mail address and sophisticated, secure, while appropriately unique password, and "*voila!*" into your e-mail inbox, you go! But wait! Before you can get into your e-mail inbox, you get a notification pop-up box that says, (paraphrasing, of course,) "Hey, just so I *really* know it's you, I'm going to send you a code to your phone, which I want you to give me before I let you in your e-mail." So, if we go back to the original description of 2FA, the 'something you know' is your password, and the 'something you have' is your phone number, which your e-mail provider will then use to send you a text containing a code that, once entered correctly, will grant you access to your e-mail. Most, if not all, e-mail providers today will have this functionality available. 2FA is a powerful tool to prevent unauthorized access to your e-mail as one of the concentric circles of protection.

When should I use 2FA? The short answer is every time a company offers the service. 2FA significantly increases the security of the account you are accessing. A note of caution with 2FA: there are times when scammers and hackers will request you provide them with the 2FA code the company or service sent to your phone or e-mail. *Never*, I repeat *never*, give this code to anyone you do not know and trust, as your account can become compromised. Most companies that provide 2FA will often add the message when sending to not share the code with any other individual in the text message containing the code itself.

What's a safer location to receive the 2FA code? Between receiving a 2FA code via e-mail or text message, I would recommend text message as the safer option. I say this because, in general, it can be more difficult for a scammer or hacker to obtain the code if it is sent directly to your phone than to an e-mail, which could have already been compromised. There are also authentication apps that can directly connect to your account, that can generate a code for access verification. This is beneficial because they do not need a phone number to which they send a code to so as to gain access to your account since the code is already generated on the app. I find, however, that the text messaging option is enough to keep my accounts safe.

What are the benefits of using 2FA? Most importantly, 2FA keeps your account secure by providing that added layer of security and verification. It also makes you a less attractive target to potential hackers since they know that accessing your accounts will be more difficult, making it likely that they would move on to other targets that may not have as much security in place. 2FA is not a foolproof system, which is an unfortunate reality we live in as a result of the interconnected world today, but in conjunction with other security measures we've discussed so far, it is an essential step in securing your accounts.

Virtual Private Network (VPN)

Virtual Private Networks, or VPNs, were initially designed for businesses to allow computers and networks to communicate securely between each machine. The necessity of using a VPN in today's environment to stay safe on the Internet has increased significantly, as it provides a secure, protected connection between your computer and the websites you are visiting. Think of VPNs like a tunnel—you are on one end of the tunnel, and your credit card provider where you are looking to pay your monthly bill is on the other. The tunnel protects your Internet traffic since you are using that secure connection.

Where should I use VPN? You could theoretically use a VPN every time you connect to the Internet. The one downside to this is, at times, because of the security of the VPN, your connection speed may slow down slightly. With this in mind, a minimum recommendation would be to use it any time you connect to an unsecured network where other people are joining. Examples of this would be coffee shops, airports, and libraries, to name a few. Unlike on a secured home network, VPNs are absolutely essential in such settings because scammers and hackers can sit on the unsecured networks, and if you don't connect via VPN, they can gain access to your system with relative ease.

What kind of VPN should I get? If you do a Google search of a VPN, you will see hundreds, if not thousands of results. All VPN services pretty much offer the same thing in varying levels of complexity. These are the items I would focus most on:

- *Fee*—Most good VPN providers will charge you a small fee to use their service. I use a VPN service (https://nordvpn.com) that costs $3.99 per month, which I consider a low price to pay for peace of mind, and knowing my personal information is secure when conducting business online, and
- *Logging*—You will want to choose a VPN provider that does not capture logs of your activity. Using a service that doesn't capture logs is essential because, if we go back to the example of paying your credit card, and if a scammer was able to access the logs of the VPN, they could collect the information that you input into the credit card provider's website and potentially steal your personal information.

Security and Anti-Virus Updates

Occasionally, your computer may inform you that updates need to be installed to ensure that the safety and performance of your computer are at optimal levels. Whenever your computer notifies you that updates are ready to be installed, you should allow the computer to perform these updates. In a best-case scenario, if your computer provides for the automatic installation of security updates, I recommend enabling that function through your computer's System settings. The software and anti-virus updates will most likely be located within your System settings on your computer. Enabling automatic updates will allow your computer to update as needed while simultaneously allowing you not to have to worry about selecting which portions of an update need to be installed.

As we've talked about previously, only install updates from your internal system. You will never receive an e-mail or notification from a website indicating that software updates are required on your system. Selecting these links may inadvertently install malware onto your computer. My recommendation is to employ the same tactics we discussed when verifying the legitimacy of an e-mail to ensuring the software updates are legitimate and coming from your system internally.

Ransomware

Arguably, one of the more unsettling and terrifying malware infections is called ransomware, where a hacker locks down your computer and all your files until you pay a ransom to have them unlocked. Ransomware is particularly terrifying because of how official it looks. In some instances, a ransomware infection in your computer will bring this window on your screen:

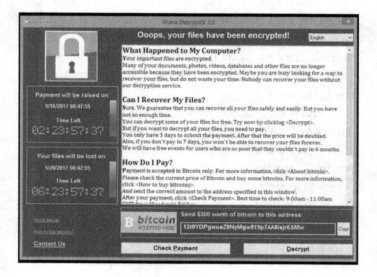

In other instances of ransomware, the screen will have the appearance being from the FBI, NSA, and Department of Justice. It will display codename hardware and accuse you of several violations of federal law. This is another example of how hackers and scammers prey on fear and dire consequences, so people will often act hastily or out of pure emotion without thinking through the situation.

What do I do? Up until recently, the FBI sent out a press release[12] stating that under no circum-

---

[12] https://www.fbi.gov/contact-us/field-offices/cleveland/news/press-releases/ransomware-latest-cyber-extortion-tool

stances should you pay the ransom to decrypt your computer. This advice is given for a couple of reasons:

1. Even after you pay the ransom, there is no guarantee you will get your files decrypted. We are talking about hackers and criminals here, who may not hold up their end of the bargain.
2. You may not get the proper decryption key from the hackers, which will render your computer, and all your files on it, useless.

In most circumstances, if you do have ransomware that has completely encrypted your computer, your best course of action is to visit an IT specialist or a local computer store that will be able to assist you with a full wipe of your computer, essentially requiring you to start all over.

Creating a Backup Point. As a generally sound practice, and probably more important should you ever become the victim of a ransomware attack, it is a good idea to store your information, files, and photos to a third-party cloud-based service, such as OneDrive, iCloud, or DropBox, to name a few. All these services allow the user to set a backup to run on a pre-determined basis, such as the middle of the night every Saturday, or a time that is convenient for you and wouldn't interrupt your daily computer activity. By backing up your information "to the cloud," in the unfortunate event your computer does need to be wiped, you will at least have a recent, backed up version, of your computer that you could pull down to prevent you from losing all your files and photos of memories with loved ones.

HELP! MY ACCOUNTS ARE COMPROMISED!

The most important thing you can do once you realize that you have a compromised account is *not to panic*. Take a deep breath, and don't be hard on yourself if you accidentally clicked on a link that you thought was legitimate. Scammers and hackers pride themselves on making e-mails and websites look as realistic as possible, and even the most thorough review of an e-mail or website may unfortunately result in a compromised account.

The first step you should take after you realize that you have a compromised account is to reset your password. By resetting your password, you are taking away the primary entry point for scammers and hackers to your account. The next step is to look at your account security questions.

As we discussed earlier, selecting answers to questions that are easy for you to remember but may not be the obvious answer to your question has already kept your account more secure than if you were to put your mother's actual maiden name. But now that you have a compromised account, a scammer or hacker already knows those answers and may, in some cases, change the questions and answers so that they can get back into your account later. So, as a best practice, I would recommend selecting different security questions and answers altogether, remembering to use the techniques that we discussed earlier.

The next step to resolve a compromised account is to review the telephone number associated with your Two-Factor Authentication if it is an account that has it enabled. Often, scammers and hackers will either disable Two-Factor Authentication altogether or change the telephone number, so, again, they can access your account and receive the security code to a number they own or know to gain entry to your account. So, if the Two-Factor Authentication has been disabled, I would recommend re-enabling the service and ensuring the phone number is your telephone number or a number that you know that can receive text messages.

Next, it is a good idea to monitor your compromised account for any suspicious activity even after taking all the steps described above. Also, you should request a copy of your credit report to determine if scammers and hackers opened any fraudulent accounts in your name as a result of your compromise. Federal law entitles you to a copy of your credit report once every 12 months for each of the credit reporting agencies: Equifax, Experian, and TransUnion. My recommendation is to spread each one of these credit reports out rather than running them all at the same time, as it is possible any fraudulent accounts opened by a scammer or hacker may not have hit your credit report yet. So, as a precaution, running one credit reporting agency every four months will ensure coverage throughout the year.

Freezing your Credit

If you have any financial accounts that hackers compromised, you can take the additional step of contacting the three credit bureaus to request a security freeze to your account. The purpose of the security freeze is to prevent any new lines of credit from being opened in your name. So, if a hacker or scammer were to attempt to open a new credit card in your name, the application would be denied, thus keeping you safe from having fraudulent accounts opened in your name.

A couple of items to remember when taking steps to place a security freeze on your account:

- A security freeze only applies to *new* lines of credit; it doesn't affect existing lines of credit
- If a scammer or hacker has your credit card information, a security freeze will not prevent them from using your stolen credit card information. In this case, you should contact your credit card company and close your current card and request a new card because of fraud.

It may be beneficial while you are in contact with the credit reporting bureaus to place a *fraud alert* on your credit report as well. A fraud alert requires the credit reporting bureau to take appropriate steps to determine if you are opening an account or if a scammer or hacker is trying to open an account in your name. The fraud alert would remain on your account even after you lift the security freeze, so your credit history is still being monitored by the fraud alerts the credit reporting bureaus set up on your behalf.

General Common Sense

One item I've touched on in almost every scenario described in this book is the use of common sense and instincts. You are your own best judge of a situation, and your instincts can tell you much about whether something does or doesn't "feel" right about a scenario. There's no harm in walking away and clearing your head before continuing, whether that be an online transaction, an e-mail you receive, or any other scenario where you are giving up your personal information. Trust your gut!

SUMMARY AND BEST PRACTICES

As a reminder, here are some best practices to keep you safe as you navigate the Internet:

- Keep your passwords robust, unique, and appropriately complex.
- Remember to walk through the steps outlined at the beginning of this book to identify a potentially suspicious e-mail before clicking any links—think 'identify before you buy!'
- The IRS will not call and demand money from you; hang up the phone.
- Do not let your emotions or fear induced by scammers' or hackers' ploys force you into an uncomfortable situation.
- Complete a regular bank statement review for potentially suspicious transactions and report any suspicious activity to your bank immediately.
- Your account security questions do not have to make sense to an outsider; they

need to be memorable enough for you to remember the answers.

- Enable Two-Factor Authentication wherever possible and use a Virtual Private Network when using an unsecured connection (e.g., library, coffee shops).
- Review steps of confirming the legitimacy of a website before entering personal information.
- Always install system and anti-virus updates to your computer when prompted, ensuring that they are legitimate updates.
- System and anti-virus updates will *not* come from an external source, such as a website or e-mail.
- If a situation doesn't feel right, walk away and revisit later.

CLOSING

T hank you for reading this book. Hopefully, the information within this book will provide you with a few tactics to fight against scammers and hackers who are looking to take advantage of you. The Internet is, unfortunately, a place where you cannot always be one hundred percent safe. The complexity and frequency with which spear phishing attacks, the creation of fake websites to steal personally identifiable information, and social engineering will only continue to evolve as additional safeguards are put in place by credit card companies and security vendors. But through constant vigilance coupled with common sense, while the Internet can be an intimidating place, implementing these techniques will assist and reduce possible instances of fraud and keep you safe as you surf.

ABOUT THE AUTHOR

Kyle is a Certified Fraud Examiner and has spent most of his career focused on fraud prevention and detection. In his free time, he enjoys golf, home improvement projects, peanut butter, and reading. Despite being a diehard Detroit sports fan, he resides in Northeast Ohio, with his wife and three children.

CPSIA information can be obtained
at www.ICGtesting.com
Printed in the USA
FSHW011352200121
77734FS